M000205355

The Tester's Pocketbook

Paul Gerrard is a consultant, teacher, author, webmaster, programmer, tester, conference speaker, rowing coach and most recently with this book – a publisher. He has conducted consulting assignments in all aspects of software testing and quality assurance, specialising in test assurance. He has presented keynote talks and tutorials at testing conferences across Europe, the USA, Australia, South Africa and occasionally won awards for them.

Educated at the universities of Oxford and Imperial College London, Paul was the founding chair of the BCS ISEB Testing Certificate Scheme and a member of the Working Party that produced BS 7925 – the Component Test Standard.

Currently, he is Principal of Gerrard Consulting Limited, a Director of Aqastra Limited and is the host of the UK Test Management Forum. He is married to Julia and lives in Maidenhead, UK.

The Tester's Pocketbook

Paul Gerrard

The Tester's Press
Maidenhead UK

Publishers note

Every possible effort has been made to ensure that the information contained in this book is accurate at the time of going to press, and the publishers and author cannot accept any responsibility for any errors or omissions, however caused. No responsibility for loss or damage occasioned by any person acting, or refraining from action, as a result of the material in this publication can be accepted by the editor, the publisher or the author.

First published in Great Britain in 2009 by
THE TESTER'S PRESS
1 Old Forge Close
Maidenhead
Berkshire SL6 2RD
United Kingdom
www.testers-press.com

The views expressed in this book are those of the author.

ISBN-10 0-95619620-9
ISBN-13 978-0-95619620-0

Typeset by Paul Gerrard
Printed and bound by Lulu.com

To My Family

Contents

Preface

Aims of the Pocketbook

This little Pocketbook has two aims.

The first aim is to provide a brief introduction to the discipline called *testing*. Have you just been told you are responsible for testing something? Perhaps it is the implementation of a computer system in your business. But you have never done this sort of thing before! Quite a lot of the information and training on testing is technical, bureaucratic, complicated or dated. This Pocketbook presents a set of *Test Axioms* that will help you determine what your mission should be and how to gain commitment and understanding from your management. The technical stuff might then make more sense to you[1].

The second aim of this Pocketbook is to provide a handy reference, an aide memoire or prompter for testing practitioners. But it isn't a pocket dictionary or summary of procedures, techniques or processes. When you are stuck for what to do next, or believe there's something wrong in your own or someone else's testing or you want to understand their testing or improve it, this Pocketbook might be of help. It will prompt you to ask some germane questions of yourself, your team, your management, stakeholder or supplier.

---

[1] Very few references to the popular testing books are given in the Pocketbook (not even to my own book). Visit the book's website testers-pocketbook.com for a 'further reading list'.

Testing is easy, isn't it?

Some people think so. Usually they are people who have never had to think about it seriously beyond it being a task on a project plan to be completed as quickly as possible before 'going live' (whatever that means). But there are good reasons why everyone should think testing is easy, or at least is second-nature. You see, everyone became a tester[2] before they could walk or talk.

Just about everything a baby can grasp is put into their mouths within seconds. It is tasted. It is *tested*. Babies and children learn incredibly rapidly through play. Play and testing are very closely related. At some level, all 'good' testing requires curiosity and imagination. So what could be hard about play?

Many things make testing hard. As we grow and mature, curiosity and imagination are often stifled and our natural testing skills are dulled. Usually, we don't test for our own benefit; rather, we test on behalf of other people whose needs, preferences, prejudices and assumptions mislead us. The things we are asked to test are not simple; systems, even small ones, can be immensely complex to understand, to configure and to interpret.

Context-neutral

Although my own background is in software testing, I have tried throughout the Pocketbook to avoid the use of terms like software, programmer, program, module etc. because testing is about so much more than software. Instead of software, I have

---

[2] From now on, I'll use the term tester to denote the role of someone who does testing. There are many testers who test full time, but testing is also a part-time role for a designers, developers and users.

used the word system to label *what* we test. I've tried to make the text as generic as possible so that it supports the testing of any system. Does this mean the Pocketbook describes the approach to testing anything? Well, that would be neat but highly unlikely.[3]

In my career, I've tested programs, software systems, interfaces, hardware, firmware, buildings, furniture, telephones, concrete and people. This Pocketbook attempts to describe the thought processes associated with testing systems in the broadest sense and is not specific to any one milieu, technology, organisation, culture. It is context-neutral.

By the way, I'll discuss testing mainly in the context of projects, but testing isn't restricted to systems development projects. Testing might also take place in a maintenance or business-as-usual environment to ensure repairs or other changes to production systems work correctly. Testing might also be used to explore how a system works for the purpose of an evaluation.

This Pocketbook won't make you a demon tester. It won't teach you anything about test process, test case design or methodology. What it will do is introduce (or remind you of) the pre-requisites, thinking processes and decision-making you need to do a half-decent job.

Test Axioms

I introduced the idea of Test Axioms in posts on my blog in the spring of 2008[4]. Over a few months their definitions evolved and in May 2008 I summarised the thinking behind them and

---

[3] If you are testing something unusual and the book helps you to formulate a test approach – please let me know.

[4] My blog can be found on my website: http://gerrardconsulting.com

tabulated 16 proposed axioms. Further evolution has occurred and with some changes, they have been used in this Pocketbook.

There was quite a reaction to the proposed axioms. Some people rejected the idea, saying there were no such things. Others were more supportive and offered new axioms or alternate definitions. You can see these posts and links to other peoples' comments on my blog.

I believe that there are a set of rules or principles that provide a framework for all testing. *But there is no single agreed definition of test.* This is mostly because every consultant and author has tended to write their own definition to suit their own purposes (and I am as guilty as the rest of them). As an industry, we are hamstrung because of this. Our clients are confused, and we get distracted by discussions on definitions because of not-invented-here mentalities and our competitive instincts. Context-neutral definitions are proposed in Chapter 1.

An axiom is something believed to be true, but cannot be proven in any practical way. It could be disproven by experiment or experience and we should be prepared to be proven wrong and welcome attempts to do this[5].

But some people object to the notion of Test Axioms and say that nothing in testing is certain. There are no axioms. All testing rules, principles, techniques, approaches etc. are heuristic. *Heuristics have value in some contexts, but are limited in application, usefulness, accuracy etc. in other contexts.* They are limited or fallible in *known* ways.

---

[5] This usage is consistent with many other famous examples: the Definitions in Euclid's Elements, Newton's laws of motion, the US Declaration of Independence present sets of beliefs without proof or corroboration. Most have subsequently been shown to be imperfect, but they continue to work for most practical purposes.

Here is my proposal for Test Axioms restated in a different way. I have tried to define them in a way that testers can, for all practical purposes, regard them as axiomatic. If anyone devises a testing context where the axioms are violated, we need to think again: Perhaps the axiom should be scrapped or changed or its scope of applicability defined.

Reviewers have generously commented on the early drafts of the book and provided many suggestions and helpful criticisms. *But so far, I have not received any concrete examples that invalidate the Test Axioms as stated in the Pocketbook.*

The Test Axioms are an attempt to provide a context-neutral set of rules for testing that identify the critical thinking processes and motivations for all test approaches.

Stakeholder obsessed

Testing is an information or intelligence-gathering[6] activity performed on behalf of (people who I will call) testing stakeholders. The manager who asked you to test could be your most important stakeholder (ask them!) They think testing is important enough to get someone as important as you involved – but might not be able to articulate why they see it as an important role.

You might use this Pocketbook to help you have a rational dialogue with them, to home in on the important issues you need to resolve to enable you to do the right job.

By the way, if you are testing the products of your own efforts, *you could be your own stakeholder*. Your approach to testing your

---

[6] In 2001, I coined the term Project Intelligence to represent the information, data, and analysed outcomes (the evidence) from testing. (Project intelligence is analogous to battlefield intelligence in a military campaign).

own products or systems will be focused on what *you and others*, as stakeholders, want to learn about those products or systems.

Most systems that need testing have stakeholders whose interests do not coincide perfectly. We cannot test everything, so we need to help them to make choices. We need to develop a good relationship with stakeholders to build consensus, buy-in and trust in our test approach. Since most stakeholders are non-technical, the language we use must be simple and direct. The Test Axiom definitions are just that.

Structure

Chapter 1 sets the scene and introduces the foundations of testing. Testing is a natural human activity; we test systems; the purpose of testing is presented. If we take an axiomatic stance to testing, we need context-, process-, technology- (and other things) –neutral definitions of test and testing. My chosen definitions close the chapter.

Chapter 2 introduces the First Equation of Testing as a way of understanding how an approach to testing can be formulated. The fundamental development process is introduced. Test Axioms, Context, Values and Thinking are presented as the building blocks of a test approach.

In Chapters 3, 4, and 5 the Test Axioms are presented under chapter headings Stakeholder, Design and Delivery respectively. Each axiom is discussed to present the reasons why the axiom exists and what its impact on a test approach can be. Some relationships between the axioms are identified.

Chapter 6 discusses how testing improvement can be achieved. The meaning of improvement and brief overviews of model-based and goal-directed improvement approaches are provided. The change-management process is introduced and a popular '8-step' process provides an example approach.

Chapter 7 provides some brief guidelines for conducting an assessment of testing in an organisation. The axioms are then listed, one per page complete with 'seed' questions for each that can help your investigations. (They could also help you to challenge your own test approach).

Chapter 8 presents some closing remarks and summarises how the Test Axioms can be used to define test approaches.

An index is included at the end of the Pocketbook. Definitions of key terms are identified by bold page numbers in the main text.

Acknowledgements

Although the writing of this Pocketbook is a solo effort, it is the concentrated result of many testing assignments starting in 1992, countless conversations with my friends in testing at the UK Test Management Forum, EuroSTAR, STAR East and West, LEWT, software testing specialist interest groups SIGIST (UK), TestNet (Holland), SAST (Sweden) and Den Norske Dataforening (Norway) and tough questioning in training courses, blogs and email discussions. You all know who you are ☺.

In particular, I'd like to thank all of the Tester Retreat attendees, especially my good friends Isabel Evans, Peter Morgan, Graham Thomas and Neil Thompson for inspiring the initial work on Test Axioms and providing feedback and guidance.

I invited a lot of people to review the Pocketbook and most reviewers responded quickly and with a lot of comments[7]. I apologise for taking so long to use them. All of the comments

---

[7] Serves me right.

were considered – some conflicted with each other and some conflicted with my aim of being context-neutral, so not every contribution made it into the final draft.

Many, many thanks to: Julien Bensaid, Bart Broekman, Bob van de Burgt, Fiona Charles, Graham Dwyer, Julia Gerrard, Derk-Jan de Grood, Tim Koomen, Alon Linetzki, Richard Marsden, Henk van Merode, Tone Molyneux, Maurice Siteur, Michael Stahl, John van Veen, Jeffrey Wannee, Adam White, Barbara van Wijk, Maarten Woolthuis and all those people who reviewed the first draft, gave verbal feedback and support. If I've omitted your name – many apologies and please let me know so I can thank you in future editions.

Susan Windsor is a most understanding business partner, advisor and friend.

Thanks and much love, as always, to my (tolerant and smarter-than-me) family, Julia, Lizzie and Max.

Any errors or omissions are my fault entirely. This is a work in progress. Please let me know how I can improve it. My email address is **paul@gerrardconsulting.com**.

Downloads, errata, further information and a reading list can be found on the book's website:

testers-pocketbook.com

A generous and elevated mind is distinguished by nothing more certainly than an eminent degree of curiosity.

Samuel Johnson

Cogito ergo pertento.

I think, therefore I test

How many testers does it take to change a light bulb?

None. We keep our testers in the dark.

1   What do we Mean by Testing?

We Test Systems

The word *system* conjures up different images to different people. To people in the IT community, a system is one or more computer applications (or sub-systems) that provide services to customers, partners or end-users. A software company might view their software product, which is a component or sub-system of larger systems as a system. But a software-centric view is rather too narrow for our purposes.

A *systems approach* takes a much broader view and a system might include the computer hardware, software and infrastructure, but might also include the procedures, partners, management, users and many other assets.

We'll use a rather abstract definition of system from now on.

A system is a combination of related parts organized into a complex whole.

A system can be anything from a mobile phone to a guided missile; a web site to a global entertainment network; an electric shaver to an airport; a team, company, culture or society.

Every system needs some testing; every test requires some disciplined thinking; testers are the people who think, and make testing happen.

We are all Testers; We are all Tested

We are all testers. We test all the time. We test drive a car before we buy it. We test our food before we swallow it. We re-read our emails before we send them. We download software and try it out before we pay for it. We try on clothes and ask for a friend's opinion before we commit. We visit and inspect houses before make an offer to buy them. We court prospective mates – we test for evidence of fitness for mating and raising offspring!

In every case, our behaviour is affected by the outcome of a test. If the outcome is negative, we don't buy, commit, swallow or even propose marriage. If we are risk-averse, if the outcome is neutral or uninformative, we might decide we need more information, new tests, and test again.

During the course of our lives, we are all tested or assessed in countless ways. We take school tests, examinations, IQ and aptitude tests; we fill in forms for tax assessments, new bank accounts and credit checks; we are subjected to health checks, eye tests and driving tests. Interns and apprentices are hired on the basis of successful completion of a probationary period.

We might not like it but on the successful outcome of these tests depend our grades, licence to drive, job offers and many other aspects of our very livelihood.

Everyone has their standards, and we all assess other people and things against them all the time. [8]

---

[8] Years ago, I was sat alone in Euston Railway Station Restaurant. A small man (he turned out to be a professional jockey on his travels) approached me and asked could he join me? We enjoyed a long, diverse conversation. As we parted I asked him why he chose to talk to me rather than one of the other travellers. He said, "Your shoes were clean and your tie is tied properly". I obviously passed his test.

The Purpose of Testing

At the most fundamental level, the purpose of testing is to gather information to learn about some aspect of a system and potentially make a decision based on the outcome of one or more tests. Consequently, testing is an information business, a people business and a business business. Let me explain.

Testers (or system builders[9], when they are testing) do not build; they do not put defects in and do not take defects out. In this respect, testers do not improve quality or add value to the systems they test. They are however, responsible for providing the most valuable information required by developers (to fix defects), project management (to understand and manage achievement) and stakeholders (to be assured). In this one respect, testing is all-powerful – it is the single source of knowledge of achievement in systems projects[10].

Testing is a people business. Most testers need excellent interpersonal skills, particularly communication skills. Testers and those who manage them need at one time or another to communicate with, negotiate with, influence and advise end users, developers, technical/environmental support, business and stakeholder management, internal and external auditors, outsource companies, customers, client services, and product managers. Interpersonal skills are, in many ways, more important than technical skills for testers.

---

[9] From now on, I will use the term developer to denote the people who build systems.

[10] I'm using Projects as the context for testing throughout the book because that is the most common context. However, testing can exist in a maintenance context or as a learning or evaluation exercise (to better understand a packaged-solution) for example. It doesn't make much difference to the thought processes involved.

A business business? Testing exists to detect defects and so protect end users, but there is a higher goal: to inform stakeholder and management decision making. The stakeholders who must decide to release, accept or reject a system and the managers who must close, delay, re-think or re-plan systems projects are critically dependent on the information produced by testers. In this respect, testers are a great ally of their stakeholders.

When we execute a test, if our aim is to understand aspects of the system under test to make a decision, we can treat the test as an information gathering or learning process. We design tests to gather specific information that we do not currently have.

The Definition of Test

It's about time I defined the most important little word in this Pocketbook.

This Pocketbook is about that word – test – used as a noun and as a verb. It's about testing as an activity and the outcome of that activity. It's about the people or organisations who commission that activity and those who use the results. Very much it's about the people who call themselves testers and the complex systems on which we work.

It's a small word, but it turns out to be a large subject. So let's get our definition right.

We need a definition of test that is context-neutral so I looked up test in the dictionary.com website. Of the many pages of references to the word test and its applications in many areas, the definition from the American Heritage Dictionary is the most appropriate.

Test: (noun) a procedure for critical evaluation; a means of determining the presence, quality, or truth of something; a trial

This statement seems to capture the essence of what is meant by a test – but there are three variations. Well this isn't so bad I think, as all three taken together give us the foundations we need. Let's take a closer look at each one.

A procedure for critical evaluation

Critical evaluation involves a skilful judgement as to the truth or merit of something. A test is a procedure, usually with a series of steps that include some form of preparation, execution, results gathering, analysis and interpretation. This isn't a definitive description of a test procedure. There could be more steps and one could break these main steps down further.

The procedure doesn't necessarily require prepared documentation, but many tests are so documented.[11] The important thing is that there is a perspicacious thought process at the heart of a test.

This thought process is driven by the need to evaluate the system under test with respect to its adequacy, consistency, behaviour, accuracy, reliability or any other significant aspect or property.

A means of determining the presence, quality, or truth of something

A test could determine the presence (or absence) of something easily enough, but quality is a different matter: the term is

---

[11] The merits and demerits of planned, scripted testing compared with ad-hoc, unscripted exploratory testing are the cause of some debate.

loaded with emotional connotations, but we are rescued by the dictionary.

A quality can be, "an essential or distinctive characteristic, property, or attribute"[12]. Now we can see that a test can reveal these properties.

Can a test determine the truth of something? Well this makes good sense too. Typically, we need to test an assertion such as, "this system meets some requirement[13]" or "this system behaves in such a way" or "this system is acceptable" and so on. There's a certain amount of subjective judgement involved but we can see that a test or tests could provide evidence for someone to exercise that judgement and make a decision.

A trial

The notion of a trial implies that the process of testing a system will help us to evaluate that system with respect to its qualities. The purpose of such an evaluation is normally to make a decision.

The decision might be to accept or reject the system, but it might also be to expose its shortcomings so they can be remedied in some way. A test might also influence an individual or organisation to change direction – to rethink a design; to relax or change a requirement; to scrap a component

---

[12] From dictionary.com. Note that I'm not using the term quality to reflect the relationship between a user or stakeholder and a product. Quality is like beauty – in the eye of the user. I won't be drawn into discussions of how one measures it. I'll avoid using the word wherever possible from now on.

[13] A requirement is a singular need of what a particular system should do. Sets of requirements may be documented in detail or at a high level, but requirements can never be complete. Implicit requirements reside in the heads of users, stakeholders, developers and testers.

and start again; to buy rather than build or build rather than buy.

A natural way of looking at a system under test is that it is on trial, and will be judged in some way.

The definition of testing

From our definition of the noun test, we can derive a verb easily enough.

Test: (verb) to critically evaluate; to determine the presence, quality, or truth of something; to conduct a trial.

So far so good[14].

---

[14] But not that good, really. Unfortunately, the testing profession is dogged with terminological problems. The words test and testing can be preceded and prefixed by countless words that qualify them. Re-test, user test, acceptance test can all be both nouns and verbs, for example! Always check the context of the words test and testing to be sure you understand what is meant by them.

2   The Equation of Testing

Deriving a Test Approach[15]

Since we are all testers, it would be convenient to imagine we could approach the testing of any system in the way that we tested as children. How nice it would be to simply pick up a system, roll it around in our hands like a toy and with our minds eye speculate on what the system does, how we might use it and how we could test it. For simple toys and the simplest systems we can do this, but real-world systems are rarely simple, unfortunately.

We'll use an 'Equation of Testing' to help us to understand how we can derive a test approach for any system. But we first have to look at why the derivation of a test approach for non-trivial systems is itself, non-trivial.

Many approaches to developing complex systems have been devised and promoted over the years. Historically, many were appropriate for projects characterised by large scale and staged development – so called Waterfall[16] methodologies. The

---

[15] I'm using the word Approach to represent the set of methods, processes, techniques, tools and whatever else is required to conduct the testing of a system from start to finish. Many people use the word Strategy; others document these approaches in Master or High-Level Test, Assurance, Quality Plans, Test Charters or site-specific documents.

[16] The waterfall model is a sequential development process, in which development is seen as flowing steadily downwards (like a waterfall) through the common stages of requirements analysis, design, implementation, testing and deployment.

majority of testing theory is based on approaches for large systems projects. But over the last twenty years or so, there has also been increasing dissatisfaction with Waterfall approaches because they tend to be expensive, bureaucratic, inflexible and slow to deliver. A large number of alternative development approaches have emerged to improve the situation. Incremental, Iterative, Agile and many variations now exist.

Where does this leave testing? Unfortunately, the testing community have not been well-served by the methodology merchants. Testing is usually under-represented in the methodologies as phases or activities that 'just-happen' or as activities that can be absorbed into development activities, leaving end-of-project user or acceptance testing as something that 'the business can work out for themselves'.

To keep pace with the continuously evolving methodology rat-race is a real challenge. In this Pocketbook, we'll look at some first principles that I believe underpin all testing thinking. It turns out that evolving a test approach isn't as daunting as it seems.

Fundamental Development Process

The fundamental process of development and test is set out in the simple diagram over the page.

The define-build-test[17] sequence is universal among all methodologies. It can be applied to any project deliverable whether it is a document, a component, a sub-system or the complete system. It is a simplification of course, but the

---

[17] In this context of define-build-test, the word 'test' is shorthand for running a test or running many tests. When I want to identify that activity explicitly, I'll use the phrase 'test execution'.

essential relationship between the three activities is unchanging.

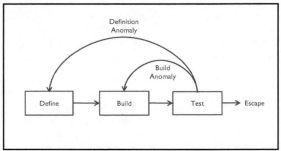

Figure 1 the fundamental development process

There are three outcomes of the testing activity:

- The first feedback loop is where a test exposes an anomaly in the definition of the system under test. In this case, perhaps a rethink of the problem or the design of the system is required.

- The second feedback loop is where a test exposes an anomaly in the build of the object. In this case, the developer needs to fix a defect and resubmit the system for re-testing.

- The third outcome is where tests pass successfully. It delivers the required evidence that the system is ready for use; it is acceptable.

Of course there are complications not reflected in this simple model. Three obvious ones are missing:

- The test environment or set up is wrong and the tests are invalid or impossible to run. Testing might be suspended until the environment or set up is corrected. In extreme cases the test might be abandoned.

- The test might expose defects with the definition or build that are so severe that a major rethink of the definition or rebuild of the system is required. The system is not acceptable.

- The testers run out of time. A decision needs to be made on whether the system is good-enough to proceed or a time extension is required for more testing.

The structure of most projects requires testing to be conducted in stages. Typical projects involve multiple definition documents to be written and reviewed. Small components are built and tested individually. Tested components are built into sub-systems and tested. Sub-systems are assembled to create the full system and tested as a whole. Finally, tested systems are installed in a more realistic environment with real users operating the system using appropriate procedures.

In this Pocketbook, we won't look at the detailed logistics of staged tests. Rather we'll focus on the knowledge required to derive a test approach to meet the needs of our testing stakeholders.

The First Equation of Testing

After such a lengthy introduction, I had better show you the first equation of testing[18].

AXIOMS + CONTEXT + VALUES + THINKING =APPROACH

What does this mean? The equation isn't an equation in the mathematical sense of course. What it suggests is that in order to derive an approach to testing in our context we need to take account of three key aspects, and do a lot of thinking.

---

18 At least, I believe it is the first. Please let me know if you know of another.

The Equation of Testing is my attempt to unify the thinking relating to Test Axioms and the differing approaches appropriate to both similar and different contexts. The equation is just a basic recipe. Importantly, the equation is intended to apply to all approaches and to all testers.

Let's take these four ingredients in turn.

Test Axioms

This Pocketbook promotes the view that formulating a test approach is primarily a thought process. The next three chapters introduce the critical thought processes required to formulate a testing approach using terse, but accessible, axiom definitions. The axioms 'divide and conquer' the knotty problem of defining a test approach.

In the context of designing a testing approach, a Test Axiom is something we believe to be self-evident and we cannot imagine an exception to it. For example, *Testing Needs Stakeholders* is axiomatic because it makes no sense to plan or execute testing if no one is interested in the outcome. How or why would we test in the absence of stakeholders?

The Test Axioms are intended to trigger the thought processes required to formulate a test approach.

Context

By context, I mean the overall project, organisational, technical and cultural world that surrounds our system and activities and has an influence on the way we need to test. Most importantly, this includes the stakeholders to whom we are accountable. The list below is split into some constraints and opportunities, but this categorisation is but one of many. Most items on the list can be constraints *or* present opportunities, of course. One project's constraint can be another's opportunity.

Constraints	Opportunities
• Culture	• Early testing
• Technical environment	• Communication
• Process	• De-duplication of effort
• Timescales	• User Involvement[19]
• Available people, skills	• Test automation
• Contracts, budgets etc.	

Stakeholders obviously have a special place in our context. They bring two most important aspects of context to our testing:

- Stakeholder goals: these are the overall goals that the system, when implemented, is intended to achieve. Goals can be very high level such as saving the company money, increasing sales, launching new products. But they can be lower-level or business-supporting goals such as providing better management information, merging two systems into one, replacing an old system with a new one and so on.

- Product risks: Products represent the intermediate and final deliverables of a project. Product risks relate to the definition of the system, the stability (or lack) of requirements, the complexity of the system, and the defect-proneness of technology which could lead to failures[20]. Product risks represent the ways in which

---

[19] In the IT community, the term user denotes someone who actually makes use of or operates the system. From now on, I'll use the label to denote anyone who uses, operates, depends on or participates in the system to be tested.

[20] A failure occurs when a system fails to behave the way we (or our stakeholders) require it to.

intermediate products or the final system could fail or be defective.[21]

Goals and product risks are fundamental to testing. Put very simply: testing, where possible, must demonstrate that stakeholder goals can be met, and that product risks have been mitigated.

Values

Organisations and individuals bring a set of values that will influence their choice of test approach. Typically, these will relate to the levels of formality, documentation, structure, autonomy that they are accustomed to (and comfortable) using. The values of testers and the values of the project or stakeholders may be different. Project and stakeholder values are part of context. We, as test practitioners, bring our own set of values to the project.

Testers having different values are likely to propose different approaches to testing in the same context. If our values align with those of our project and stakeholders the proposed approach should be an easier sell and good fit to the problem at hand. If our values are not aligned we might be regarded as being too radical or too conservative. The fit might not be good and we may have a harder time convincing people that our approach is sound. Companies offering testing services or training will obviously be more successful in working with client organisations whose culture and values match their own.

---

[21] I have adopted the product, process and project classification of risks. Project risks are risks related to the external dependencies and influences of a project. Process risks are risks related to the internal management of a project. Product risks are those of most interest to testers.

Unsurprisingly, different practitioners favour working in different contexts and so they tend to specialise in their preferred context. Testers familiar and comfortable with safety-critical systems would probably be uncomfortable working in a start-up developing a rapidly evolving social networking web site – and vice-versa.

Thinking

I've used the term thinking to represent the group of activities required to derive the approach. This will involve consideration of the current context, investigation and questioning of stakeholders, business experts, analysts and developers and technical support teams.

It is the context that makes every project unique but naturally, companies have their preferred ways of working. There may be conventions, policies, standards that we are expected to follow. It is important to find out which of these must be used, which can be adapted and which can safely be ignored.

Many development projects in user organisations are enhancements to existing systems. Much of the required thinking may already have been done for us in previous projects and is part of our context. Some of this thinking can be reused safely, although the compromises made in the last project might not be appropriate this time around. We must think carefully what we need to achieve and how much of this thinking can actually be reused to help us achieve our aims.

Ultimately, the outcome of testing is focused on the stakeholders. The process of how to build consensus on a test approach won't be considered here, but sensibly, the stakeholders should have the final say on what is most appropriate to their purposes.

Communication

Usually it is best to research a bit, think a bit, feedback to and invite feedback from our project and stakeholders. In this way, we can check that we are headed in the right general direction and we are achieving buy-in throughout the process.

Once the thinking part is over the outcome of our thinking needs to be communicated to our project. Our approach needs to be articulated to the stakeholders and other project participants. A number of formats can be used but it should come as no surprise that in larger projects, voluminous word-processed documents are the norm.

However, the essence of a test approach can be communicated in just a few pages. Consider using a Test Strategy-*lite* format for stakeholders and put the voluminous detail into a larger document with an index that identifies which sections are suggested-reading for each stakeholder or project role.

3 Stakeholder Axioms

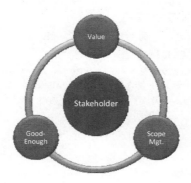

Stakeholder

Testing needs stakeholders

What is a stakeholder?

A tester's stakeholders are those people who have an interest in the outcome of tests, and the information that testers provide. They could be the individuals or organisations who:

- Are funding the project.

- Are affected (in a beneficial or detrimental way) by the new or changed system.

- Contribute to the project as e.g. designers or developers[22].

- Need to make key decisions to keep the project moving forward (e.g. project or business managers).

- Are custodians of the new system (asset managers, service management staff).

- Are or represent the user community (business users, customers, partners or society as a whole).

As the tester, we need to identify and engage the people or organisations that will use and benefit from the evidence we are to provide. If we don't do this how can we answer the following questions?

- What should (and should not) be tested?

- What are the most important (and least important) things to test?

- Who will use the evidence we generate from testing?

- What information do they need?

- How will we squeeze all this into the time available?

If we have no stakeholder, no one will take any notice of the outcome of our tests so there is little point in doing any testing. We won't have a mandate or any authority for testing. We won't get the resources or time we need. We can't report test execution passes or failures or lodge enquiries with any expectation of them being answered by anyone.

Who are the stakeholders and what do they want? There are four types of stakeholders based on their needs:

---

[22] If you are a designer or developer, testing your own work, you should think about what you, as your own stakeholder, need from your own tests.

- Sponsors: these stakeholders need evidence that the system can support their business goals and the risk of failure of the system is bearable.

- Users: these stakeholders need evidence that the system will 'work' for them.

- Project Management: these stakeholders need to know exactly the status of deliverables with respect to their availability (are they built?), to their acceptability and defectiveness. If there is a problem, the manager may need to re-plan or at least manage expectations.

- Designers and developers: these stakeholders need to know where their products fail – so they can fix defects or adjust their designs.

Stakeholders must articulate *what* evidence they need the testers to produce. This will start with the business goals and the product risks of most concern. The testers need to know what information is required from the test process. Often this will take the form of documentation, but in some projects paper documentation may be minimal.

Communications between the team in general may focus on information provided on shared spreadsheets, simple requirements/incident tracking tools or whiteboards visible to all. Exactly how the evidence is provided needs to be agreed with stakeholders.

Testers are *accountable* to stakeholders. As a consequence, most of the axioms encourage you to engage, consult, refer to and defer to stakeholders. Our stakeholders are our customers, directors and supporters. Our test approach should focus our energy and the testing effort towards meeting their needs at all times.

Testers should be Stakeholder-Obsessed.

Value

The value of evidence is for the stakeholder to decide

Every test should have value to stakeholders. The tests that we run have value to stakeholders in that they provide evidence to support decision making in four ways:

- Evidence that the system will meet the business goals of the project.

- Evidence that the system will not fail or if it does, that the impact of failures is bearable.

- Evidence to reproduce and diagnose failures and repair and re-test the failed system.

- Sufficient evidence to support decision-making.

If a test has no value – then why are we preparing it or running it? Decisions on Scope (p20), the choice of Test Models (p25), and approach to Prioritisation (p38) must reference the needs of and be authorised by our stakeholders.

Scope Management

If we don't manage scope, we may never meet stakeholder expectations

If the mission of testing is to satisfy the needs of stakeholders with respect to the evidence they require to support decision making, the aspects of the system to be tested needs careful identification. The scope of testing is the highest level definition of what is to be tested. Different projects will define scope in different ways but we must expect some or all of the following to be included:

- The business goals and the processes, procedures, hardware and software systems that are being built to attain those goals.

- The training, preparation, readiness etc. of the individuals, teams, partners or organisations who will collaborate, operate, support and use the system.

- The product risks to those business goals of most concern.

We must work out a way of managing the definition and agreement of the scope of testing. If we do not have an agreed scope:

- How will we focus our efforts on the aspects of the system that are most important? We might spend lots of time testing trivial features at the expense of critical ones.

- Stakeholders may assume we are testing everything – and when we have not, and things fail – who will be accountable?

It is essential that stakeholders understand and agree what will and will not be tested. The way we specify the items in and out of scope will be, for example, an inventory of project deliverables, products or system features. This could be as informal as a list on a whiteboard or as formal as a one-thousand page specification.

However formal or informal our project is, change is inevitable. Change can bring new things to our attention that we need to test and remove other things we might already have tested. Change can disrupt the work of testers dramatically, so we have to make sure that stakeholders are aware of the impact and any change in the scope of our testing.

Good-Enough

The scope of testing and acceptance are always compromises

The acceptance decision will always be made on incomplete evidence.

In the real-world, compromise is inevitable. The challenge for testers is to provide sufficient evidence for stakeholders to make their decisions using their judgment in a rational and informed way.

The phrase 'Good Enough'[23] has been used in the context of acceptance decision making and comprises a set of simple criteria to be observed by stakeholders. If X is our system, stakeholders might accept the system if:

1. X has sufficient benefits.

2. X has no critical problems (that we know of).

3. The benefits of X sufficiently outweigh the problems.

4. *In the present situation*, and *all things considered*, improving X would cause more harm than good.

5. All the above must apply.

To expand on this rather terse definition, 'X (whatever X is) has sufficient benefits' means that there is deemed to be enough of this system working for us to take it into production, use it and benefit by using it. It has no critical problems, i.e. there are no severe defects that make it unusable or unacceptable. At this moment in time, with all things considered, if we spend effort

---

[23] James Bach, http://www.satisfice.com

trying to perfect X, that effort is probably going to cost us more than shipping early with the known problems.

This framework allows us to release an imperfect system early because the benefits may be worth it. But how does testing fit into this good-enough idea?

Firstly, have sufficient benefits been delivered? The tests that we execute must at least demonstrate that the system features providing the benefits are delivered completely.

Secondly, are there any critical problems[24]? Our test evidence must show where critical and non-critical problems exist. There should be no critical problems for it to be good enough.

Thirdly, is our testing good enough to support this decision? Have we provided sufficient evidence to say these risks are addressed and those benefits are available for release?

Who makes the decision?

The tester should not make the acceptance decision. Rather, the tester provides the evidence. It's a bit like being an expert witness in a court of law. An expert witness may be asked to give their evaluation of the guilt or innocence of the defendant but they will usually refrain from doing so, as their expertise relates to the status and interpretation of evidence and not the outcome of the trial.

Sometimes, however, stakeholders are naïve. They might not have the clearest vision of their goals or perhaps they find it hard to articulate their concerns. So, we might be asked to give an opinion on whether a system is acceptable or not. The best response is to re-present the evidence as we see it; summarise

---

[24] In this context, critical problems are those that make the system unacceptable. It's a bit of a tautology, but you need to get stakeholders to think seriously about how they would define a 'critical problem'.

the evidence of benefits, of known problems and the outstanding risks. Stakeholders should appreciate that the benefits and risks are their concern not ours and we should be recognised as an honest broker.

But sometimes we are asked for our opinions to help stakeholders to decide. We need to be very sure to communicate why we say what we do and reference stakeholder goals and risks as best we can. When things go well, we might get a pat on the back. But if things go badly once the system is in use we can be sure our opinions will be remembered.

In general, testers should avoid taking acceptance decisions on behalf of stakeholders. It is far better to be an information provider and trusted advisor than be a stakeholder by proxy.

4 Test Design Axioms

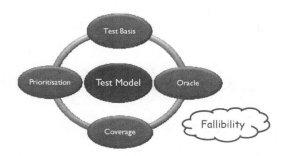

Test Model

Test design is based on models

Testing is a process in which we create mental models of the environment, the system, human nature, and the tests themselves.[25] Test design is the process by which we select, from the infinite number possible, the tests that we believe will be most valuable to us and our stakeholders. Our test model helps us to select tests in a systematic way.

Test models are fundamental to testing and the next few pages are dedicated to a discussion of them.

---

[25] Paraphrased from Software Testing Techniques, Boris Beizer, 1990.

What is a test model?

A test model might be a checklist or set of criteria; it could be a diagram derived from a design document or an analysis of narrative text. Many test models are never committed to paper – they can be mental models constructed specifically to guide the tester whilst they explore the system under test.

We use test models to:

- Simplify the context of the test. Irrelevant or negligible details are ignored in the model.

- Focus attention on a particular aspect of the behaviour of the system. These might critical or risky features, technical aspects or user operations of interest, or particular aspects of the construction or architecture of the system.

- Generate a set of unique (within the context of the model) tests that are diverse (with respect to that model).

- Enable the testing to be estimated, planned, monitored and evaluated for its completeness (coverage).

From the tester's point of view, a model helps us to recognise particular aspects of the system that could be the subject of a test. The model focuses attention on areas of the system that are of interest.

We usually base models on one of the following sources:

- The test basis – we analyse the text or diagrams or information that describe required behaviour.

- The architecture of the system – we identify testable items in its user-interface, structure or internal design.

- Modes of failure – we identify potential ways in which the system might fail that are of concern to stakeholders.

- Usage patterns – we focus on the way the system will be used, operated and interacted with in a business context.

An example of a test model

Suppose we want to test how a car (an automatic gearshift model) accelerates from rest to its top speed and check that it meets our performance objective (e.g. from a standing start to 60 mph in 8 seconds). We might model this system as:

1. A gas pedal or accelerator that can have a variable position.

2. A power source (the engine) having a power output varying from a minimum to a maximum value dependent on the gas pedal position.

3. A mass (of the whole vehicle and driver) acting at a defined centre of gravity – which accelerates according to Newton's second law.

4. Formulae that relate the gas pedal position, power output and acceleration.

We can extract all the information we need for our model from the design document for the car.

Using the model, we could design a test like this: "From rest, set the pedal to maximum power for a period of ten seconds. Use our formulae to calculate a predicted speed for every second of acceleration. Compare the actual speed with predicted speed every second of the test."

When we conduct the test in a real car we compare its speed at every second to that predicted by the model. In this way, we could determine whether the car meets its performance objective.

If the system under test (the car) does not behave correctly according to our model we either change the car, or we change the model (our interpretation of the car's behaviour).

Everything looks fine – doesn't it?

Models may over-simplify the situation

But in the real test, our car may not behave as we expect because our model ignores several key aspects of the car's behaviour and context. We might reasonably ask:

- Would a real driver be as aggressive or gentler with the gas pedal?

- What is the wind speed and direction?

- What are the road conditions (wet, dry, tarmac, dirt etc.)?

- What load is the car carrying, beyond the driver?

- Is the car on a level road, an uphill or downhill incline?

- What is the power efficiency of the system?[26]

Our model is grossly simplified, incorporates many implicit assumptions and would need significant refinement to be an accurate representation of a real car under test. *All models simplify the context of tests to varying extent.* The challenges are to select models that are an *accurate enough* representation of our system under test and to interpret the test outcomes obtained *with care*.

In general, all test models, even those proposed by textbooks are heuristic, in that they are useful in some situations but are always incomplete and fallible. Before we adopt a model, we need to know what aspects of the behaviour, design, modes of failure or usage patterns the model helps us to identify and what assumptions and simplifications it (explicitly or implicitly) includes.

---

[26] Even applying an efficiency rating would be a gross over-simplification. Typically, 80% of the power generated by burning gasoline is wasted heating the car and atmosphere, overcoming friction of car components, tyre wear and wind resistance.

Formal test models

Formal models tend to be derived from analyses of design or requirements text, tables or diagrams or are derived from the architecture or structure of the system itself. These models are often specified (and sometimes mandated) in standards or development methodologies. They are intended to be systematic methods that, when properly used by testers, deliver equivalent sets of tests from the same test basis and context.

In principle, a quantitative coverage measure can be obtained from a formal test model. But see the section on Coverage (p35).

Informal test models

Test models don't necessarily have to be diagrammatic or represent the requirements or design of the system. For example, some models are just lists of modes of failure, risks or vulnerabilities.

Security hackers and criminals adopt patterns of attack to undermine or breach the security of software systems. To verify that systems are not vulnerable, security testers use lists of vulnerabilities as a model to trigger ideas for tests.

Other informal test models include navigation paths through business processes or the system itself, quality criteria, user roles and behaviours or scenarios that stakeholders believe are relevant to the use of the system in the real world.

Informal models cannot be used to define quantitative coverage measures.

Ad-Hoc test models

Some models can be ad-hoc, invented by the tester just before or even during testing. If, while testing, a tester sees an opportunity to explore a particular aspect of a system, he might use his experience to think up some interesting situations on-the-fly. Nothing may be written down at the time, but the tester is using a mental model to generate tests and speculate how the system should behave.

Stakeholders may not tell testers to use specific test models, but where documentation written by, on behalf of or approved by stakeholders is used to derive tests (the Test Basis), the stakeholders ought to be aware of what models are adopted and how tests are being derived. The stakeholders may be of the opinion that the model generates too few (or too many) tests to be meaningful or economic.

Test Basis

Testers need sources of knowledge to select things to test

The Test Basis is the source, or sources, of knowledge required to select what aspects of our system we might test and how we might test them.

The documentation for a system such as the requirements or design will define the required behaviour, internal design or structure and other characteristics of the system. This documentation will be used by the system developers to guide the construction of the system.

Since this documentation describes what the system should do and perhaps how it should do it, it is an obvious source of knowledge for identifying things to test, short of using the system itself. Accurate, complete, up-to-date, consistent documentation can provide much of the Test Basis.

A test basis requires more than documentation

But documentation rarely provides a complete description of the behaviour of a system and we need to supplement documentation with other sources of knowledge.

It is possible that we are given a system without a specification to test. This is common if the system under test is a packaged solution or COTS[27] product. In this case, there may be little, if any, documentation available that describes the behaviour of the system other than its user guide. In this case, we will probably have to resort to using the users' business process as a basis for testing or use our exploratory instincts.

Of course, the system itself is a source of knowledge and to a large extent, we can explore it to learn what it does and model its behaviour in the context of the users' need.

Some systems may be so complex that the *only* way to test is to behave like users, in which case, we may need to understand the different roles or stereotypes that are appropriate. As a tester, we will need to model the users' behaviour in some way and use this as the test basis and our test model.

Stakeholders must recognise the test basis

The test basis is the source of knowledge that must be recognised by the stakeholders so they trust that the right information is being used to inform the testing. The test basis may include documents written by or on behalf of stakeholders, but this is not always the case. Sometime we have to create a test basis from multiple sources including our own or other people's experience.

---

[27] Commercial off the Shelf. Packages and COTS are ready-built products that require configuration. Customers may require changes to the packages themselves, but this is typically a risky business – testing and (regression testing) becomes a critical factor.

Whatever the sources of knowledge used as the test basis, the stakeholders must be aware of and approve them. Stakeholders and testers must also understand that all test bases are partial and Fallible (p41).

Oracle

Testers need sources of knowledge to evaluate actual outcomes or behaviours

A Test Oracle is the source, or sources, of knowledge that enable us to predict the outcome of any test. In effect, an oracle tells us what a system does in all circumstances and situations. Implicitly, if an oracle does this, it is perfect. Our oracle might be the same sources as the test basis. Whatever our sources of knowledge are, like test bases, they are fallible.

We use oracles to define expectations

When we execute a test, we obtain an outcome, but we need to determine whether the outcome meets expectations. When we compare the test outcome to that predicted by our oracle there are two possibilities:

- If the outcome matches expectations, it meets, in an incremental way, a user's need or requirement. The test incrementally increases our knowledge and confidence.

- If the outcome does not match expectations, it does not meet, in an incremental way, a user's need or requirement. The test will incrementally increase our knowledge but decrease our confidence (until the system is fixed and re-tested successfully).

Each test generates a discrete quantum of evidence. When all tests are run, we aggregate these quanta of evidence and take a more rounded view of the situation. See the Event Axiom (p51).

There is no limit to the variety in which systems can behave, so testers must be prepared to capture and/or observe the outcomes of significance and recognise those that do not match expectations.

Oracles are more than documentation

A requirement or design document may define the required behaviour of a system to some extent but it will never define all its possible behaviours. It is completely impractical to define all of the required behaviour (and forbidden behaviour) of a system[28]. Consequently, our test oracle will comprise more than documented requirements. It must include some received wisdom, experience and selected heuristics that are meaningful to stakeholders.

Suppose there is no oracle. The outcome of a test cannot be evaluated in any reliable way. Outcomes can never be recognised as correct or anomalous at all. They won't even register as interesting or intriguing! Without an oracle or oracles, the outcomes of testing simply pass us by.

Some systems are built and documentation comes later; some systems will never be documented; yet others (almost all) systems have gaps in documentation. It is never possible to totally rely on documentation as our oracle. As a consequence, we always need to place some reliance on stakeholders and users directly, our common sense and experience to support documentation oracles.

---

[28] A complete requirement would include *ALL* of the behaviours of a system for example the status of every element, attribute or feature at all moments in time. Further, it must include all the prohibited behaviours for every feature. Usually, prohibited behaviours are defined 'system wide' or are presumed to be conventional – and many are overlooked by system developers as a consequence.

Scripted or unscripted tests?

There is some dispute over whether expected outcomes should be documented in test scripts. Advocates of planned, pre-scripted testing argue that without a script, testers won't stay focused on the task in hand and that feasible, but erroneous outcomes might be accepted by the tester. Advocates of unscripted testing say scripts force testers to check only what the script tells them to; they may be blind-sighted to other erroneous outcomes and their testing creativity is constrained. There is evidence for both points of view.

Testing contexts vary and the appropriate level of test scripting varies too. At one extreme, scripts can define every single step in a test procedure in detail. At the other extreme, there are no scripts, perhaps just a single phrase mission statement or mini-plan for a brief session of exploratory testing[29]. Between these extremes, an approach comprising a blend of scripted and unscripted tests, agreed with stakeholders, is usually required.

There is no formula for the balance of scripted and unscripted testing. Some stakeholders and contexts will demand that tests are pre-scripted. In other contexts, test scripts have marginal value. Discussions about which is most appropriate will focus on time spent scripting versus time spent testing, cultural values and personal preferences.

---

29 Most easily defined as simultaneous learning, test design and test execution. See http://en.wikipedia.org/wiki/Exploratory_test for a fuller discussion and references.

Coverage

Testing needs a test coverage model or models

Formal test models and coverage

Coverage is the term we use to describe how we assess the thoroughness or completeness of our testing with respect to our test model. Ideally, our test model should identify coverage items in an objective way. A coverage item is something we want to exercise in our tests. When we have planned or executed tests that cover items identified by our model we can quantify the coverage achieved and, as a proportion of all items on the model, express that coverage as a percentage.

Formal coverage targets are referenced in some industry standards and often used in project test plans. To be compliant with such standards or plans, these coverage targets must be met. Identifiable aspects of our test model, such as paths through flow charts, transitions in state models or branches in software code can be identified and used as the coverage items.

But models and coverage items need not necessarily be defined from industry standard models. *Any model* that allows coverage items to be identified can be used.

For example, a graphical model that includes blobs and arrows could be used to define two basic coverage targets:

- All blobs coverage

- All arrows coverage

- And so on

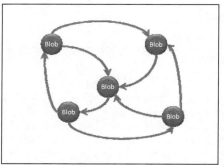

Figure 2 Example of a graphical test model

The principle is this: a formal method allows coverage items to be reliably identified on the model. A quantitative coverage measure can therefore be defined and used as a measurable target.

Informal test models and coverage

Informal models tend to be checklists or criteria used to brainstorm a list of coverage items or to trigger ideas for testing or for testing in an exploratory testing session. These lists or criteria might be pre-defined or prepared as part of a test plan or adopted in an exploratory test session.

Informal models are different from formal models in that the derivation of coverage items is dependent on the experience, intuition and imagination of the practitioner using them so coverage using these models can never be quantified. We can never know what 'complete coverage' means with respect to these models.

Needless to say, tests derived from an informal model are just as valid as tests derived from a formal model if they increase our knowledge of the behaviour or capability of our system.

Using coverage to manage testing

Coverage measurement can help to make testing more manageable. If we don't have a notion of coverage, we may not be able to answer questions like, 'what has been tested?', 'what has not been tested?', 'have we finished yet?', 'how many tests remain?' This is particularly awkward for a test manager.

Test models and coverage measures can be used to define quantitative or qualitative targets for test design and execution. To varying degrees, we can use such targets to plan and estimate. We can also measure progress and infer the thoroughness or completeness of the testing we have planned or have executed. But we need to be very careful with any quantitative coverage measures or percentages we use.

A coverage measure (based on a formal test model) may be *calculated* objectively, but there is no formula or law that says X coverage means Y quality or Z confidence. All coverage measures give only indirect, qualitative, subjective insights into the thoroughness or completeness of our testing. There is no meaningful relationship between coverage and the quality or acceptability of systems.

Coverage and objectivity

Quantitative coverage targets are often used to define exit criteria for the completion of testing, but these criteria are arbitrary. A more stringent coverage target might generate twice as many items to cover. But twice as many tests costing twice as much, does not make a system twice as tested or twice as reliable. Such an interpretation is meaningless and foolish.

Sometimes, the formal models used for the definition and build of a system may be imposed on the testers for them to use to define coverage targets. At other times, the testers may have little documentation to work with and have to invent models of their own. *The selection of any test model and coverage target is somewhat arbitrary and subjective.* Consequently, informal test models and coverage measures can be just as useful as established, formal ones.

The table below summarises how formal and informal test models and coverage measures should be regarded.

Model Definition	Coverage Measure	Interpretation
Formal, objective	Quantitative	Subjective
Informal, subjective	Qualitative	Subjective

Prioritisation

Testing needs a mechanism for ordering tests by value

In any non-trivial system, the number of tests that could be run is (effectively) infinite. Compare this huge number of tests to the number of grains of sand on a beach. Our challenge as testers is to identify, from the myriad of possible tests, the 'pinch' that are the most valuable and that there is time to execute.

We need a way of comparing tests so that one test may be ranked above another so the former is retained and the latter (potentially) discarded.

We must invite stakeholders to take a utilitarian view[30]. In principle, we could put prices on the value, cost and facility of our tests but the reliability of calculations based on these numbers is highly dubious. Nobel prizes have been awarded to researchers into Choice Modelling Theory[31] but this approach

---

[30] Utilitarianism proposes that humans make choices based on their wish to maximise happiness and comfort and minimise unhappiness and pain and so on.

[31] Daniel McFadden, http://emlab.berkeley.edu/users/mcfadden/

is more appropriate to large groups such as consumers or voters.

Small groups of stakeholders will make choices using mysterious processes influenced by prejudice, politics, personal preferences and subjective perceptions of unreliable data. We need to prioritise somehow – so what are we to do?

Stakeholders make the value judgements

We need to let stakeholders make the value judgements or agree with us a set of criteria to allow us to make them by proxy. These value judgements or criteria will inevitably align with the ways that evidence supports the Good-Enough decision-making process (p20).

Since the stakeholders may be funding the project in part or whole, they are best placed to take the balanced view on the value and priority of any test.

The tester's contribution

Testers make two contributions to the prioritisation effort:

- We need to assess the potential cost and ease by which tests can be run. Many tests may look similar, but some are complicated, require complex setup, large scale environments, tools or large teams and/or be very expensive. Consequently, a test may have great value, but its cost or other constraints may make it infeasible.

- It is likely that groups or patterns of tests (derived from particular features of the system or based on the outcome of selected test models) need to be compared. We must provide the background required for the stakeholders to understand the content and value of these groups of tests.

Prioritisation in stages

Prioritisation starts right at the beginning of our project and continues to the point where we execute tests. In general, prioritisation takes place at three stages:

- Scoping (p20): we select (prioritise) some aspects of the system to be tested and others not to be tested.

- Design (p25): test models focus attention on selected aspects of our system (and exclude others).

- Execution (p47): time for test execution is limited but we need to execute the most valuable tests first (prioritisation again).

Although Stakeholders set the rules, it is likely that we, the testers, actually make the choices of which tests are to be retained and which are to be discarded at each of these stages.

A note on test constraints

The items listed as constraints on p13 are considerations in our prioritisation effort:

- Culture: can our people work this way? Formal approaches may not allow for high test volumes; practitioners may baulk at high ceremony, for example.

- Technical environment: is it technically and economically possible to create an environment to support our tests?

- Process: does our process allow (e.g. by being strict or flexible enough) for the execution of our tests?

- Timescales: is there time enough to include these tests?

- Available people, skills: do we have the people? Do we have the requisite skills in the team?

- Contracts, budgets etc: does our contract or agreed budgets preclude these tests?

Fallibility

Our sources of knowledge are fallible and incomplete

Testers are completely dependent on having sources of knowledge to test. These sources of knowledge will usually include some or all of the following:

- Written documentation.

- Verbally communicated knowledge and advice.

- Experience of using similar systems.

- Experience of using the current system (that is to be replaced).

- Personal intelligence, intuition, perception, beliefs, and prejudices.

All of our sources of knowledge are fallible and incomplete because they are created by human beings who are prone to human error[32]. Although our brains are wonderfully adept at interpreting fuzzy data for the purpose of catching mammoths for dinner, we are much less good at communicating in a formal, precise way and interpreting what we perceive without error.

Our knowledge and the methods we use are partial and imperfect. For example, Test Bases (p30), Test Models (p25), Oracles (p32) and Prioritisation (p38) are all prone to error. It is only sensible to allow for this in our thinking, communications and actions.

Human errors can have an adverse impact at any stage of projects and these errors are the primary cause of defects in the systems we test. The evidence that we produce and more

---

[32] I use the words error and human error interchangeably.

importantly, the analysis and interpretation of that evidence by stakeholders is just as prone to error also. The selection and filtering of our sources of knowledge, the methods and models we use and the interpretation of results needs careful consideration qualification and dispassionate, critical thinking[33].

What significance can stakeholders place on the evidence produced by testers and testing? It will always be subjective, but the confidence that stakeholders have in that evidence will be maximised by engaging them early and involving them in discussions of scope, prioritisation, test models, coverage and so on.

---

[33] Wikipedia: Critical thinking is purposeful and reflective judgement about what to believe or what to do in response to observations, experience, verbal or written expressions, or arguments.

5 Test Delivery Axioms

Confidence

The value of testing is measured by the confidence of stakeholder decision making

The Good-Enough axiom (p22) summarised the need to provide enough evidence to support decision making with confidence. The value of testing evidence is determined by how confidently stakeholders can make the required judgements.

Of course, confidence cannot be quantified and neither can the value of our testing. This can only be assessed by the people using the evidence produced by or test efforts. To ensure we provide good value, we need to look at how we build confidence in stakeholders.

Confidence that goals are met

On the one hand, the test evidence must demonstrate in a range of scenarios that the goals of the system are met. The tests must align with the expectations of stakeholders in that they must reflect how users will use the system in familiar, conventional and relevant ways. The test outcomes should then provide the required confidence (assuming the system passes the tests). Early and ongoing buy-in to our test approach will maximise our chances of success so our first question to stakeholders is:

"What do we need to demonstrate to you to make you confident that the system will meet your business goals?"

The answer to this question will help us to manage scope and select test models to ensure we meet their expectations.

Confidence that the risk of failure is low

On the other hand, the tests must also provide evidence that the system does not fail badly. Any anomalous behaviour of the system can cause concern, but our ambition must be to select tests that attempt to expose the failures of *most* concern. If these tests pass, concerns are reduced. If they fail we can diagnose the defects that cause the failures, repair them and repeat the tests to show the repairs work correctly.

If we are to conduct tests that demonstrate that failures do not occur, we need to understand what the risks of most concern in the minds of stakeholders actually are.

The challenge for testers is to engage stakeholders in the (possibly uncomfortable) discussion of potential failure. Some potential modes of failure may be avoided by careful design but all the failure modes of concern will need testing to provide evidence and confidence to stakeholders. The proposed tests must be negotiated with stakeholders and the question asked, "Will these (and these, and these...) tests address your concerns adequately?"

We need to initiate (and possibly facilitate) early discussions to assess the risks of failure. By understanding modes of failure, we can enumerate them and use them as coverage items to be exercised in tests. By defining these modes of failure, we can articulate tests that demonstrate these modes of failure are less likely[34].

Again, early and ongoing buy-in to our test approach will maximise our chances of success. Our second question to stakeholders is therefore:

"What do we need to show you to make you confident that the system will not fail in ways that you fear?"

The answer to this question will help us to manage scope and select Test Models to ensure that we address their concerns.

Confidence that "we've tested enough"

Our third question to stakeholders is almost inevitably:

"How much evidence is required to give you confidence?"

It would be helpful to have some form of confidence metric associated with the evidence we provide – but this is a forlorn hope. No such metric can ever exist.

Instead, we have to rely on subjective judgements of scope, test models and coverage measures and test evidence to build confidence. In all our discussions of goals, risk of failure and coverage, the buy-in of stakeholders must be sought continuously.

---

[34] When planning, designing or executing tests, it is likely that new concerns will emerge as we learn more. Risks assessment and management is an ongoing activity.

Repeat-Test

Some repeated tests are inevitable

When a test is run, it generates some evidence of the system working or not working or working in a different way, or it exposes interesting or anomalous behaviour that might require further investigation.

If a test has passed, and the system (or its environment) were never to be changed, what value would there be in running that test again? *The value of running the same test twice (or more) on an unchanged system or environment is marginal.*

However, repeated testing is inevitable because tests don't all pass and systems and environments do change over time.

Re-Tests

If our system fails a test, certainly the system and possibly its design would need to change to correct the anomaly. A repeat run of the test that failed would be required to demonstrate that the changes have had the desired effect – by achieving a test pass.

These tests are called re-tests. Re-tests are essential because they are the only direct way of obtaining evidence that defects in a system have been correctly repaired.

Re-tests are tests that when last run – caused a failure.

Regression Tests

When a system is changed (to pass a failed test or to meet a new or changed requirement), it is possible (and often likely) that a change in one part of the system will caused a problem in another part of the system. Having run and passed our re-tests, we might re-run other tests to verify that the unchanged parts of the system still work correctly.

Sometimes a tested system or a reliable system in production needs to be relocated to a different environment. In both cases the working system might fail in the new environment if its design is sensitive to change. We usually re-run some tests to verify that the unchanged system still works correctly in the new environment.

Regression tests are tests that when last run – passed.

Always plan to repeat some tests

Repeat testing is inevitable because:

- Systems rarely pass tests first time and need to be fixed. (Re-tests are required).

- Systems can be very sensitive to change and regressions are likely. (Regression tests are required).

If repeat testing is inevitable, we should never be surprised at the need for it. This does not mean we take a pessimistic view. Will the system be perfect first time? Will this system never change? – The answer to both these questions is usually No.

We should always make some allowance in our plans to cover re-test and regression testing – even when we have grounds for being optimistic that the system will work and never change.

Execution Sequencing

Run our most valuable tests first – we may not have time to run them later

It makes sense to deliver the most valuable evidence as soon as possible:

- Our Stakeholders need to receive the most valuable evidence as soon as practical so they can make their decisions sooner and with more confidence.

- By and large, it is better to correct defects in systems as soon as possible to minimise rework where other deliverables are affected. It is better to run tests that are likely to expose severe defects early to maximise the time available to fix them.

- The third reason for sequencing tests in a particular order is that the time available for testing may be limited or squeezed. It is sensible to sequence tests so that the most valuable tests are run if execution time is limited, if testing starts late and deadlines are fixed, if testing takes longer than planned or if testing is stopped prematurely.

If we don't sequence tests in this way, it is possible that when testing does stop, we may find that some worthless tests have been run at the expense of more valuable ones.

Logical constraints on sequencing

There may be practical difficulties in sequencing tests of course. It is not possible to test a whole system before it has been assembled from its components. Components are usually most efficiently tested in isolation and the developers are best placed to do this work. So it would make no sense to promote whole-system testing before component testing.

In a staged project, testing tends to align with the deliverables that become available at each stage. Requirements, designs and components are delivered in sequence, so the testing of these products is staged accordingly. Staged testing is, in effect, a sequencing mechanism in-the-large.

Logical test sequencing

Mechanisms for sequencing tests are similar to those for prioritisation, but logical constraints, such as those mentioned above must be taken into consideration.

Tests are often grouped into sequences that follow a mode of operation or business process. In this case, dependencies force the sequence and this sequencing cannot be avoided.

The sequencing of tests might be forced upon us because later tests may depend on the outcomes of previous tests. In an accounting system, management reporting or reconciliations require data captured in previous tests to be available for control and reconciliation reports to be meaningful.

As usual, we must ensure stakeholders understand what mechanisms for sequencing have been used. If we run out of time and valuable tests are not run, we may be asked to explain why.

Environment

Test execution requires a known, controlled environment

Our test model makes an implicit, critical, simplifying assumption: that our tests will be run in a known environment.

What is an environment?

All systems need to be tested in context. What this means is that for a test to be meaningful, the system to be tested must be installed, set up, deployed or built in a realistic environment that simulates the *real world* in which the system will be used.

In the context of testing, a realistic environment would replicate all of the business, technical and organisational environment. Much of this environment comprises data that is used to drive business processes, provide reference data and the configuration of the system itself.

But perfectly realistic environments are usually impractical or far too expensive unless we are testing very high criticality systems such as aeroplanes, nuclear reactors or brain scanners.

Almost all testing takes place in environments that simulate, with some acceptable level of compromise, the real world[35].

Cars are tested on rolling-roads, in wind-tunnels, on vibration-beds and private test-tracks before they are tested on the open road. Computer systems are tested in software labs by programmers and software testers before end-users are engaged to try them out in a production-like environment.

Getting realistic environments to test in

Simulated environments are fallible just like our test-bases and test models, but we just have to live with that. We need to be careful to stage tests that are meaningful in the environments we have available and that test outcomes really do mean what we interpret them to mean.

The reliability of test outcomes is dependent on the environment in which tests are run. If a test is run in an environment that is incorrectly set up:

- A test that fails may imply the system is defective when in fact it is correct.

- A test that passes may imply the system is correct when in fact it is defective.

Both situations are highly undesirable, of course.

Getting environments set up and delivered in time

Test environments can be difficult and expensive to set up and maintain. Often, just when support teams are working on the new production environment, the testers demand test

---

[35] But there is compromise even in so-called "High-Consequence" systems. Tests on aeroplanes use crash-test dummies, not passengers; nuclear reactors are simulated (with software); wax effigies might be used to test brain scanners.

environments (and perhaps several of them). Late in projects, there always seem to be competing demands on support teams.

Environments may be delivered late, or not at all, or they are not configured or controlled as required. Inevitably, this will delay testing and/or undermine the stakeholder confidence in any evidence produced.

The general rule must therefore be: Establish the need and requirements for an environment to be used for testing, including a mechanism for managing changes to that environment – *as soon as possible*.

Event

Testing never goes as planned; evidence arrives in discrete quanta

When we think about testing and how we might test, we may uncover interesting anomalies in the test basis, invent novel test models or expose new modes of failure that need attention. *But it is only when we execute a test and analyse its outcome that we obtain evidence of the actual behaviour of our system.*

But events blow governments and the best laid test plans off course[36].

Each test generates a discrete quantum of evidence when run; evidence builds up as we execute more and more tests. We can predict the outcome of these events ahead of time using our oracle but can never *know* what *will* happen[37]. The actual

---

[36] "Events dear boy, events" was Harold Macmillan's response to a journalist when asked what is most likely to blow governments off course.

[37] If we 'know' the outcome of a test before we run it, why run it?

outcome of tests is highly dependent on the reliability of the system, the testers, the test environment, test data, our test models and test basis.

Test execution plans are uncertain

The Fallibility axiom (p41) tells us our sources of knowledge are undependable. The tester is a human being and prone to error. The system is being tested because we are uncertain of its behaviour or reliability. As a consequence, *the plan for any test worth running cannot be relied upon to be accurate before we follow it.*

Predictions of test status (e.g. coverage achieved or test pass-rate) at any future date or time are notional. The planning quandary is conveniently expressed in the *testing uncertainty principle*:

- *One can predict test status, but not when it will be achieved;*

- *One can predict when a test will end, but not its status.*

Consequently, if a plan defines completion of testing using test exit criteria[38] to be met at a specified date (expressed in terms of tests run and the status of those tests) it is wise to regard them as planning assumptions, rather than hard targets.

- If exit criteria are met on time or earlier, our planning assumptions are sound: We are where we want to be.

- If exit criteria are not met or not met on time, our plan was optimistic: Our plan needs adjustment, or we must relax the criteria.

Whichever outcome arises, we still need to think very carefully about what they actually mean in our project.

---

[38] In test plans exit, closure, acceptance and completion criteria are names for criteria to be met to deem test execution to be complete.

How do we estimate test execution?

From the discussion above, you might think that the question, 'how long will these tests take to run?' is a foolish one. But project managers need to plan so we cannot avoid being asked.

The best we can do is to set out, in the time allocated with the resources available, the tests that could be prepared and the tests that could be run. Since test failures require diagnosis and possibly rework and re-testing by developers, any estimate for testing needs to include an allowance for diagnosis and rework (and re-testing) by developers and re-testing by the testers.

Of course, it may be that the resources and time allowed for testing has already been defined for us. Perhaps the project has a fixed deadline, or the development and test activities are timeboxed[39]. In this case, the estimation task is to determine what can be achieved in the time available.

If we have knowledge and experience of similar projects, perhaps we can make an allowance for the difficulty in getting environments set up, running tests, the number and nature of failures, time taken to fix and the time and success rate of re-tests.

These estimates can never be reliable before testing begins. But, if we monitor progress closely when the test activities start, there's a good chance that we will learn enough to refine our estimates and re-align our plan as time passes. Even so, estimation is always an uncertain process.

---

[39] Timeboxing is a time management technique common in planning projects, where the schedule is divided into a number of separate time periods (timeboxes), each period having its own deliverables, deadline and budget.

Incident management

We need to keep track of test execution progress (tests executed, test pass/fail status, coverage achieved etc. etc.) but we also need a mechanism for managing and communicating the unplanned events that have a bearing on the successful delivery of test evidence.

We hope that our tests pass, but we know that test failures are possible at any time and we must allow for them. Test failures cause additional, unplanned work for both developers and testers, so it is important to track these events so the additional work can be delegated, monitored and controlled.

Unplanned event tracking is usually called incident[40] management.

Unplanned events can stop testing or adversely affect our plans and cause delay to testing and defect fixing or undermine our tests. An agreed incident management process – even if it is informal, will allow the response to the inevitable but unplanned events to be more considered.

Never-Finished

Testing never finishes; it stops

In earlier chapters we discussed how there is no upper limit to the amount of testing we could do (p38), that our sources of knowledge are fallible (p41) and that ultimately, acceptance is a compromise (p22).

In every project, the time arrives where testing stops. If all tests have passed, all defects have been repaired and re-tested and

---

[40] Incidents are also called observations, anomalies or problems in some organisations.

regression tests complete successfully in planned timescales, with all evidence captured – a positive acceptance decision might be a formality. But this happy outcome is a rare event.

Usually, the allocated time for testing runs out[41]. There are surely more tests that we could have run; there will probably be defects that have not yet been diagnosed, fixed and re-tested; some defects might not be worth fixing.

We hope that our test plans complete but we must be prepared to report to stakeholders on the basis of incomplete test results.

Managing test progress and stakeholder expectations is a subtle art. If testing is incomplete, the best we can do is assure stakeholders that the best testing has been done in the time available and present the evidence as it stands. Stakeholders must base their decision on the Good-Enough principle (p22).

But it may be that we cannot provide stakeholders with the evidence they need because we have been working to an unrealistic plan. If we manage scope and prioritise in a rational way, at least when testing stops we will have delivered the most valuable evidence we could have.

It's really about avoiding sudden drops in confidence late in the project. We have to manage the expectations of stakeholders and the only way to do this is to engage them early, communicate regularly and honestly, share the good news and the bad, and ensure they are as well-informed as possible.

---

[41] I'm not being pessimistic – it just seems to be to most common outcome (of over-optimistic planning, we have to assume).

6 Evaluating and Improving Testing

Do we want to improve the way we test? A silly question – of course we do. At a personal or organisational level, of course we would all like to do a better job. But a better job – compared to what?

Two questions arise:

- What does *improve* actually mean?

- How do we achieve *improvement*?

Process-model-based improvement

Quality and process improvement approaches that have worked for manufacturing and other process-intensive industries for many years have been adapted for systems development organisations. These approaches have similar characteristics:

- A ranked hierarchy of practices which are assigned increasing levels of 'goodness' in a process maturity model.

- Processes are assessed against the model; 'better' practices are explicitly identified from the model.

- By adopting better or mature processes, the quality of the systems we produce using them – will improve[42].

---

[42] A leap of faith? Comparative studies of the cost-effectiveness of 'good' practices in different contexts are thin on the ground.

Various process improvement models have been formulated along these lines and used over the years.

These approaches focus on benchmarking (measuring) processes against a model and using the model to identify process improvements. Improved process is the goal; achieving higher benchmark scores is the method.

One criticism of model-based approaches to process improvement is that the models discourage thinking and innovation[43]. The solution to our problem is always provided by the model – wherever we are on the maturity model, the next thing to improve is prescribed.

Process-model-based improvement can work for organisations with a heavy process focus, but most system development and testing is performed in the context of projects and project-based activities seem to need a different treatment.

Goal-directed improvement

Projects are characterised by their goal-driven, unique, dynamic, temporary nature. If our aim is to improve testing in projects, we need to be goal-oriented rather than process-oriented. Perhaps the best we can do is to identify *what* could be improved; the *how* – we must let practitioners make their own choices.

Improvement of project performance must be founded on the need to achieve project goals more reliably, faster and more economically. Therefore, testing improvement must be driven by the same needs.

A complicating factor for testing is that testing does not improve the systems that are tested. The purpose of testing

---

[43] Painting by numbers does not usually lead to great art. Talent, innovation, individualism are usually ignored by process models.

was discussed very early in the Pocketbook (p3) – testing is essentially an information provision service. That information has Value (p20) to stakeholders so it seems obvious that our goals in any testing improvement initiative must be:

1. To increase the value of the information we provide.

2. To provide valuable information sooner.

3. To provide valuable information more cheaply.

Any improvement must be assessed against these three goals.

Using the axioms to evaluate testing

This Pocketbook advocates the use of Test Axioms to focus on critical thought-processes of testing. Each axiom suggests that there is a thought-process required to understand our context and how best to approach the testing challenge in our current project. The axioms suggest *what* should be thought about and where a choice could be made, but not *how* it is done or which choice is best.

The axioms do not prescribe best practices[44] because they are context-, process-, technology-, and practice-neutral. They can be regarded as simple one-liners to trigger a thought process. They do not represent a test process model. They are a model of the essential thinking processes required to test. That's all.

If we want to improve our testing, we should treat the axioms as a list of choices that must be made in our approach to testing. Those choices are strongly influenced by the context of our projects, culture and the values of our organisation. The axioms are a set of starting points for our thinking – not a recommendation.

---

[44] There are no *best* practices in a discipline used in such a broad range of contexts and industries as ours - only *appropriate* ones (for a context).

When we look at our own or someone else's testing, we use the axioms to identify some of the choices that must be made in a test approach. If a choice suggested by an axiom is missing, or we cannot understand why a choice is made, a choice was made without thinking, or a poor choice was made, we may be onto something important in our assessment.

Test assessment by enquiry

Now, if the axioms represent a set of necessary thought processes required for testing, then the axioms naturally prompt us to ask certain questions. A children's rhyme give us our cue:

> *I keep six honest serving-men*
> *(They taught me all I knew);*
> *Their names are What and Why and When*
> *And How and Where and Who.*

> *The Elephant's Child*, Rudyard Kipling.

On the pages that follow, each Test Axiom is presented on its own page for reference. The axiom is stated as a headline with a brief paragraph of explanation. The consequence if an axiom is ignored or violated the consequences are presented.

The questions that appear against each axiom are suggestions only to get us going. We can use Kipling's six servants to generate more. *The aim of the axioms is to stimulate thinking – not to do the thinking for us.*

Some axioms seem to be most appropriate to large systems projects perhaps, *but they could also apply to the very next test we need to plan, create or execute.* If the axioms really are universal, then they should be useful from a tester's, test manager's or stakeholder's point of view.

Making change happen

Our assessment will identify some areas where a test approach or its execution by an organisation or individuals is lacking. Whether we use a process-model approach or we simply ask questions and reason that certain changes will improve matters, our next step is to facilitate a transition from the 'old way' to a 'new way'. This process is usually called change management.

According to Wikipedia, Change Management is a structured approach to transitioning individuals, teams, and organizations from a current state to a desired future state.

Many, many books have been written on the subject – and there are many consulting firms offering change management services, methodologies and support. There is no single, guaranteed approach, but the critical challenge is to get people who need to change to:

- Believe that the old way is bad and the new way is better.

- Commit to transitioning from the old way to the new way.

Many methodologies have been suggested but a very popular one is John Kotter's 8-step process[45]. For our purposes, I've adapted it slightly and summarise the stages in the table below.

Whether we use Kotter's 8-step process or another, the important thing is to recognise that change is a human process, not a technical one. Providing evidence that change is good, writing new processes and giving training is never enough.

---

[45] John Kotter, "Leading Change".

Step	Activities
Mission	Identify why things 'are the way they are'; establish a sense of urgency; define the mission
Coalition	Create the steering team
Vision	Use the outcome of the assessment to set out the road map of change; create the plan
Communication	Articulate and communicate the vision at all levels
Action	Provide resources, remove the barriers, delegate authority
Wins	Demonstrate achievements to maintain momentum
Consolidation	Suppress resistance, look for new opportunities
Anchoring	Embed changes into the culture

The people who must undertake the transformation process must believe they are moving to a 'better place'; they need support before, during and after the transformation. The transformation will not be complete until it is embedded in the culture.

The recommendation must be to select a change management process from the many available and adapt it to our culture; we should use our own internal language and terminology. We should not miss a step, and need to make sure our change sponsor 'sticks with the programme'.

7 Conducting a Test Assessment

Although we will research test documentation and records, most information will be gathered through interviews of key staff. This chapter provides brief guidelines for interviewing and the following pages provide some 'seed questions' listed under each axiom.

Planning Interviews

- Ask management to give us a list of appropriate interviewees at all levels of the organisation. It is better to start with the most senior and work downwards.

- Interviews with senior managers tend to be shorter but more focused – allow 30-45 minutes.

- Interviews with junior staff may take longer, if we find interviewees particularly helpful. Allow 45-60 minutes.

- Try and get all the interviews scheduled to complete in less than two weeks. Three interviews per day are comfortable; more than three per day can make it hard to keep up with note-taking and assimilation.

- If helpful, write a brief note that introduces us, our objective and agenda. Send to all prospective interviewees so they can prepare.

- Prepare a list of the questions we'd like answered – we'll keep this as our checklist.

Conducting Interviews

- We'll have an agenda, but we'll be flexible:

    - Introduce ourselves, the objectives of our assignment and agenda.

    - Ask the interviewee to introduce themselves and walk through their role as if telling a story.

    - Use our checklist to ensure we get what we need.

    - If the interviewee cannot answer, we ask them to email us later or suggest the name of another source.

    - What problems (relevant to the scope of the assessment) does the interviewee have?

    - What might be potential solutions to the problem?

    - Do they have any questions to ask us?

    - Advise them of our next steps and how we intend to feed back our assessment, and timetable.

What questions should we ask?

We can use the questions on the following pages to seed our enquiries into the test approaches in use. Many of them make good interview questions – most of them are open questions that require more than a yes or no answer. Obviously, some questions are more appropriate for managers than practitioners – and vice versa.

Interviewees may be nervous about answering our questions. They may feel that they are under investigation or under suspicion and their professional competence is in question. We need to assure them that there is no hidden agenda.

We must also always treat information gathered in interviews with sensitivity and respect the privacy of the individuals concerned.

Stakeholder

Testing needs stakeholders

Summary

Identify and engage the people or organisations that will use and benefit from the test evidence we are to provide.

Consequence if ignored or violated

There will be no mandate or any authority for testing. Reports of passes, fails or enquiries have no audience.

Questions

- Who are they?
- Whose interests do they represent?
- What evidence do they want?
- What do they need it for?
- When do they want it?
- In what format?
- How often?

Value

The value of evidence is for the stakeholder to decide

Summary

The outcome of a test and the way evidence is presented defines its value, regardless of its source.

Consequence if ignored or violated

The approach to testing is an end in itself. The test evidence generated lacks relevance, is ignored, is misunderstood, is inappropriate and has little value to the people that matter.

Questions

- What acceptance decisions must stakeholders make?

- What evidence do stakeholders need to make these decisions with confidence?

- When can the required evidence be gathered?

- Who needs to provide subject-matter expertise to inform the testing (and make it valuable)?

- Who are best placed to perform these tests?

- Are the people or organisations nominated to perform the tests capable of doing so?

- What environment and infrastructure is required to make the testing meaningful and valuable?

Scope Management

If we don't manage scope, we may never meet stakeholder expectations

Summary

Testers need to identify and agree the items in and out of scope and manage change of scope over time.

Consequence if ignored or violated

Stakeholders assume 'everything' will be tested. Tests outcomes of no interest to stakeholders are reported.

Questions

- How do stakeholders define the scope of the system and what needs testing?

- What sources of knowledge are available to define and understand scope in detail?

- What are the (likely) drivers for change?

- How will testers accommodate changes of scope?

- How will testers analyse the impact of change of scope?

- Do testers have the authority to resist or challenge change?

- How will defect fixes be assured (through re-testing)?

- How will testers test changes?

- How will testers communicate the status of changes?

Good-Enough

The scope of testing and acceptance are always compromises

Summary

Stakeholders and testers must jointly appreciate that there is no limit to testing and that the acceptance decision will always be made on incomplete evidence. In fact, acceptance may occur in spite of evidence, based on information known only to stakeholders.

Consequence if ignored or violated

Stakeholders are frustrated by poor system quality or late delivery because their expectations are unrealistic. Testers are frustrated because they cannot finish testing, the system is imperfect and stakeholders decide to accept regardless.

Questions

- How much evidence from testing will be required to make the acceptance decision?

- Who is authorised to make the acceptance decision?

- What is the mechanism for assessing the value of evidence gathered during testing?

- What coverage model(s) can be used to judge that enough evidence has been gathered?

- What criteria will be used to judge that the system under test is acceptable or unacceptable?

Test Model

Test design is based on models

Summary

Choose test models to derive tests that are meaningful to stakeholders. Recognise the models' limitations and the assumptions that the models make.

Consequence if ignored or violated

Tests design will be meaningless and not credible to stakeholders.

Questions

- Are design models available to use as test models? Are they mandatory?

- What test models *could* be used to derive tests from the Test Basis?

- Which test models *will* be used?

- Are test models to be documented or are they purely mental models?

- What are the benefits of using these models?

- What simplifying assumptions do these models make?

- How will these models contribute to the delivery of evidence useful to the acceptance decision makers?

- How will these models combine to provide sufficient evidence without excessive duplication?

- How will the number of tests derived from models be bounded?

Test Basis

Testers need sources of knowledge to select things to test

Summary

Identify and agree the sources of knowledge required to identify what to test. Use multiple sources; compare them and cross-check.

Consequence if ignored or violated

There is no way of knowing what to test. Inconsistencies and gaps in knowledge cannot be identified.

Questions

- What sources will be used to describe the system and identify what is to be tested?

- What is the derivation/heritage/provenance and reliability of these sources?

- What are the levels of authority or precedence of these sources?

- How can test outcomes be related to the goals and concerns of stakeholders?

- Who will authorise the use of these sources of knowledge?

- Who will arbitrate/resolve conflicts between these sources of knowledge?

- Who or what will provide the knowledge covering gaps in these sources?

Oracle

Testers need sources of knowledge to evaluate actual outcomes or behaviours

Summary

Identify and agree the sources of knowledge required to determine expected outcomes. Use multiple sources; compare them and cross-check.

Consequence if ignored or violated

There is no way of knowing whether a tested system behaves correctly or not. Inconsistencies and gaps in knowledge cannot be identified.

Questions

- What sources of knowledge should be used to derive expected outcomes to validate observed behaviour?

- Do stakeholders approve the use of these sources as a test oracle?

- What confidence can we have in these sources?

- Do expected outcomes need to be documented prior to test execution?

- What is the derivation/heritage/provenance and reliability of these sources?

- What are the levels of authority or precedence of these sources?

- In case of dispute, who or what source will be the final arbiter?

Coverage

Testing needs a test coverage model or models

Summary

Testers need a means of assessing the thoroughness or completeness of testing with respect to the chosen test models in ways that are meaningful to stakeholders.

Consequence if ignored or violated

Stakeholders do not understand the status of testing. No one knows what has been tested, what has not been tested or if testing is finished.

Questions

- How will coverage definitions that describe the thoroughness or adequacy of testing be articulated?

- Can these coverage definitions be used to define a quantifiable coverage measure?

- How can the coverage measures be related to the goals and concerns of stakeholders?

- Could these measures support estimation, planning and progress reporting?

- How will the thoroughness/adequacy of testing be articulated to stakeholders?

- With respect to the acceptability of the system, what interpretation(s) of these coverage measures could be made?

Prioritisation

Testing needs a mechanism for ordering tests by value

Summary

Testers need to be able to rank tests in order of value and identify which tests are the most valuable.

Consequence if ignored or violated

Stakeholders do not get the evidence they require to make decisions because the necessary tests have not been executed in time.

Questions

- Who is authorised to define the priorities to be used to select things to test?

- How will the priorities be articulated?

- What are the constraints on testing in the current context?

- Who is authorised to impose, change or remove these constraints?

- Who will authorise the inclusion or exclusion of tests during scoping?

- Who will authorise the inclusion or exclusion of tests during test design?

- Who will authorise the inclusion or exclusion of tests during test execution?

Fallibility

Our sources of knowledge are fallible and incomplete

Summary

Test Bases, Models, Oracles and Prioritisation approach are fallible because the people who define and use them are prone to human error.

Consequence if ignored or violated

Confidence in the meaning, thoroughness, accuracy and value of tests is misplaced.

Questions

- How have the sources of knowledge required for testing been identified?

- Who is responsible for the content in these sources?

- Has the content of the sources been agreed unanimously?

- Have these sources stabilised?

- Have these sources been verified against other references or validated against the experience of contributors and other stakeholders?

- What measures can be taken to minimise the impact of error in our sources of knowledge?

- If sources are fallible or conflict, who or what is the final arbiter?

Confidence

The value of testing is measured by the confidence of stakeholder decision making

Summary

Testers must understand the relationship between test evidence and the decisions that stakeholders must make. Testing should focus on providing the evidence that stakeholders require to make decisions with confidence.

Consequence if ignored or violated

Stakeholders regard the evidence produced by testing as irrelevant, unreliable, incomplete and not aligned with their goals.

Questions

- What evidence do stakeholders need to make decisions with confidence?

- How will stakeholders use that evidence?

- How are the goals of testing articulated in plans, specifications, meetings and other communications?

- How will we ensure that evidence is delivered as early as practical to stakeholders?

- How will we assure the accuracy and currency of the evidence produced?

- What preferences for format, detail, frequency, precision, accuracy exist for the evidence produced?

- How will the evidence be transmitted, acknowledged and reviewed by stakeholders?

Repeat-Test

Some repeated tests are inevitable

Summary

Define and agree a policy for re-testing and regression testing; make an allowance for repeat-tests in estimates and plans.

Consequence if ignored or violated

Tests to confirm that defect fixes work correctly are not run. Tests to confirm that defect fixes do not cause unwanted side-effects are not run.

Questions

- Under what circumstances will failed tests be re-run?

- Under what circumstances will passed tests be re-run?

- What criteria will be applied for the retention of tests for reuse?

- Under what circumstances will retained tests be discarded or amended?

- For the purpose of planning, how will the following be estimated or defined:

    - The proportion of tests that fail?

    - The time required for defect fixing and re-testing?

    - The proportion of tests to be used for regression purposes?

Execution Sequencing

Run our most valuable tests first – we may not have time to run them later

Summary

Sequence tests to ensure the most valuable tests are run if execution time is limited or testing is stopped.

Consequence if ignored or violated

Stakeholders do not get the evidence they require to make decisions because the required tests have not been executed.

Questions

- What criteria for selection and/or prioritisation will be applied to sequence the planned tests?

- What criteria for selection and/or prioritisation will be applied to sequence unplanned or ad-hoc tests?

- What are the constraints to sequencing tests?

- How will dependencies between tests be minimised and managed?

- Under what circumstances can tests run out of sequence?

Environment

Test execution requires a known, controlled environment

Summary

Establish the need and requirements for an environment and test data to be used for testing, including a mechanism for managing changes to that environment – in good time.

Consequence if ignored or violated

Environments are not available in time or are unsuitable for testing. This will delay testing or cause tests to be run in the wrong environment and undermine the credibility of evidence produced.

Questions

- Who is responsible for the acquisition, configuration and support of test environments?

- What assumptions regarding test environments do our test models make?

- How will requirements for test environments be articulated, negotiated?

- How will the validity and usability of test environments be assured?

- How will changes to environments be managed, consistent with changes in requirements and other deliverables under test?

- How will the state of environments, including backed up and restored versions be managed?

Event

Testing never goes as planned; evidence arrives in discrete quanta

Summary

Acknowledge the testing uncertainty principle, and manage stakeholder expectations. Agree a mechanism for managing and communicating events that have a bearing on the successful delivery of test evidence.

Consequence if ignored or violated

Stakeholders are surprised at the outcomes and progress of testing and blame the testers. Unplanned events stop testing, cause delays, upset plans and undermine the evidence produced.

Questions

- How does the test approach accommodate unplanned events?

- How do plans articulate the uncertainties and expectations of test execution?

- How will changes to the test bases, system or environment be managed?

- How will test failures be communicated, tracked and managed?

- How will unplanned events having an adverse effect on testing be recorded, tracked, analysed and reported?

Never-Finished

Testing never finishes; it stops

Summary

Recognise that testing is usually time limited and may not complete. Manage the expectations of testers and stakeholders accordingly.

Consequence if ignored or violated

Testers are frustrated that testing is stopped early. Stakeholders lose confidence and are reluctant to make decisions based on incomplete evidence.

Questions

- Are stakeholders aware that testing probably will not complete in planned timescales?

- Do testers appreciate that all tests might not be run, that the acceptance decision may be made on incomplete evidence and that the accepted system could be imperfect?

- Are testers prepared to inform, advise and facilitate the acceptance decision?

- What role will the testers have in presenting test evidence and completion (or incompletion) status?

- How will the testers support stakeholders in judging the relevance/significance of inconclusive evidence?

8   A Final Word

A tester's job will never be easy. The systems we work with vary in scale, cost and complexity by three or four orders of magnitude. Systems development projects vary in timescales and the pressures on participants. The technologies we test are changing all the time. The cultural and organisational environments we work in are human systems – the most diverse, complex, sensitive and challenging systems of all.

Process-heavy methodologies, technically dazzling tools and agile approaches work well in the right context but all have shortcomings: high ceremony, cost, maintenance and ineffectiveness; poor productivity, reliability, accountability and return on investment. We've seen it all.

Our projects are unique in scale, scope and context, so our chosen approach needs to be infinitely flexible or perfectly suited to our context. At the same time, we testers are accountable for the work we do. It seems to me that to have any chance of success, we must use our critical faculties to challenge received wisdom and pre-defined approaches and *design the test approach for every project*, almost from scratch.

We need to think, innovate, negotiate and compromise our way through the problems of testing. If there are no best-practices – *the best we can do is select existing practices or invent new ones that are appropriate for our current context.*

The Test Axioms in this book are intended make the testing challenge less scary. By focusing on the choices and thought processes required to prepare and agree a test approach they divide and help us to conquer this terribly difficult problem.

I sincerely wish you the best of luck!

Index

Are You Interested in Training?

Paul Gerrard has been providing training courses since 1992. These range from basic, testing essentials and certification courses, through to technology-specific, methodological and advanced courses. All non-certified courses are offered in a workshop format.

Certified Courses

The following certified courses (including exams) are offered:

- ISEB/ISTQB Foundation Course in Software Testing

- ISTQB Advanced Test Analyst

- ISTQB Advanced Test Manager

Customised Courses

We have accumulated a vast range of training material over the years and are pleased to compile custom courses for clients' specific needs at no extra charge. Let us know what you are looking for, and we'll create a course syllabus list with you.

Aqastra

Paul is also Co-Director, with Susan Windsor, of Aqastra (**aqastra.com**) which provides (re-)training courses focused on practical, hands-on skills including Project Survival Skills, Excel Record-Keeping for Testers, Linux for Testers, Exploratory Testing, Critical Thinking Skills, Interpersonal Skills for Testers, SQL for Testers, Supplier Management as well as week-long team-based testing projects using real software applicationsin a safe, realistic test environment.

Further Information

Contacting the Author

Should you have any questions or wish to discuss any of the issues raised in this Pocketbook, or perhaps you would like help in improving testing in your organisation, please feel free to contact Paul Gerrard.

Email: **paul@gerrardconsulting.com**

Tel: +44(0)7940 547894

Ordering copies of the Tester's Pocketbook

Additional copies of this Pocketbook can be ordered from the Gerrard Consulting website:

http://gerrardconsulting.com

(The Pocketbook can also be ordered from Amazon and other online book stores).

Custom versions of the Tester's Pocketbook

If you would like a customised version of the Pocketbook for your team, I'm happy to create one for you. Perhaps you want include company information or policy in the Pocketbook? The material in customised Pocketbooks will remain copyrighted to its respective authors.

Do get in touch if this is of interest to you.